WARRIOR
WISDOM

WARRIOR
WISDOM

Over 200 Inspirational Quotations from the Greatest Military Leaders

ARRANGED BY NICK BENAS, USMC

 hatherleigh

WARRIOR WISDOM

Text Copyright © 2023 Nick Benas

Library of Congress Cataloging-in-Publication Data is available.
ISBN: 978-1-57826-896-2

COVER DESIGN BY CAROLYN KASPER

Printed in the United States
10 9 8 7 6 5 4 3 2 1

To Kiyon, Sloan and Ari

Contents

Introduction

CONTAINED IN THIS COMPENDIUM is a collection of the very best of warrior wisdom. Each quote has been curated from notable military leaders, stoic philosophers, military advisors, and dedicated statesmen and women admired for their leadership. Each had a way with words, but each understood that the power of words is underwritten by action and strength of character. The hope is that this collection will travel with you, making you more aware of your own inner warrior.

Feel motivated to build up your own war chest. Pick and choose. Write it on a whiteboard, affix it to your fridge, or place it at the top of your company minutes—wherever they can best serve to inspire you to act like a warrior in your day-to-day life. You can browse these quotes, share them and apply their timeless wisdom to your everyday challenges. Embracing them may be the first step to become a successful leader.

I

LEADERSHIP

OFTEN, A FEW GOOD words in the heat of battle can help galvanize and motivate troops to do the impossible. These utterances have been immortalized through storytelling, biographies, captured quotes scrolled across ticker tape, bold print in newspapers, and copycat sayings spoken in Hollywood Blockbuster war flicks.

"The greatness of a leader is measured by the achievements of the led. This is the ultimate test of his effectiveness."

—GENERAL OMAR BRADLEY,
U.S. ARMY

"I have become so great as I am because I have won men's hearts by gentleness and kindliness."

—SALADIN (AN-NASIR SALAH
AD-DIN YUSUF IBN AYYUB),
SULTAN OF EGYPT &
MUSLIM WARRIOR

"Leadership is a two-way street: loyalty up and loyalty down."

—REAR ADMIRAL GRACE
HOPPER, U.S. NAVY

"You'll never get a Purple Heart hiding in a foxhole! Follow me!"

—COLONEL HENRY P. CROWE,
U.S. MARINE CORPS

"In critical and baffling situations, it is always best to return to first principle and simple action."

—SIR WINSTON S. CHURCHILL,
PRIME MINISTER OF
GREAT BRITAIN

"He who wishes to be obeyed must know how to command."

—NICCOLÒ MACHIAVELLI,
ITALIAN DIPLOMAT

"The most important thing I learned is that soldiers watch what their leaders do. You can give them classes and lecture them forever, but it is your personal example they will follow."

—GENERAL COLIN POWELL,
U.S. ARMY

"Great powers don't get angry, great powers don't make decisions hastily in a crisis."

—GENERAL JOHN ALLEN,
U.S. MARINE CORPS

"A competent leader can get efficient service from poor troops, while on the contrary an incapable leader can demoralize the best of troops."

—GENERAL JOHN J. PERSHING,
U.S. ARMY

"Always do everything you ask of those you command."

—GENERAL GEORGE S. PATTON,
U.S. ARMY

"To get the best out of your men, they must feel that you are their real leader and must know that they can depend upon you."

—GENERAL JOHN J. PERSHING,
U.S. ARMY

"Rashness belongs to youth; prudence to old age."

—MARCUS TULLIUS CICERO,
ROMAN STATESMAN &
SOLDIER IN POMPEY'S ARMY

"I am not afraid of an Army of lions led by a sheep; I am afraid of sheep led by a lion."

—ALEXANDER THE GREAT,
WARRIOR & KING OF THE
ANCIENT GREEK KINGDOM
OF MACEDON

"You learn far more from negative leadership than positive leadership. Because you learn how not to do it."

—GENERAL JOHN J. PERSHING,
U.S. ARMY

"I do not intend for 'honor, courage, and commitment' to be just words; I expect them to frame the way that we live and act."

—GENERAL CHARLES C.
KRULAK, 31ST COMMANDANT
OF THE MARINE CORPS

"Great powers don't get angry, great powers don't make decisions hastily in a crisis."

—GENERAL JOHN ALLEN,
U.S. MARINE CORPS

"The most important thing about a commander is his effects on morale."

—FIELD MARSHAL VISCOUNT
SLIM, BRITISH MILITARY
COMMANDER

"A true leader has the confidence to stand alone, the courage to make tough decisions, and the compassion to listen to the needs of others. He does not set out to be a leader, but becomes one by the equality of his actions and the integrity of his intent."

—GENERAL DOUGLAS
MACARTHUR, U.S. ARMY

"A leader's words matter, but actions ultimately do more to reinforce or undermine the implementation of a team of teams."

—GENERAL STANLEY
MCCHRYSTAL, U.S. ARMY

"If you find yourself in a fair fight, you didn't plan your mission properly."

—COLONEL DAVID
HACKWORTH, U.S. ARMY

"A reflective reading history will show that no man ever rose to military greatness who could not convince his troops that he put them first, above all else."

—GENERAL MAXWELL TAYLOR,
U.S. ARMY

"Victorious warriors win first and then go to war, while defeated warriors go to war first and then seek to win."

—SUN TZU, CHINESE GENERAL
& MILITARY STRATEGIST

"Never give reasons for what you think or do until you must. Maybe after a while, a better reason will pop into your head."

—GENERAL WILLIAM T.
SHERMAN, UNION ARMY

"The pain of discipline is nothing like the pain of regret."

—UNITED STATES MARINE
CORPS, RECRUITING
CAMPAIGN

"The temptation to lead as a chess master, controlling each move of the organization, must give way to an approach as a gardener, enabling rather than directing. A gardening approach to leadership is anything but passive. The leader acts as an 'Eyes-On, Hands-Off enabler who creates and maintains an ecosystem in which the organization operates."

—GENERAL STANLEY
MCCHRYSTAL, U.S. ARMY

"The tranquility that comes when you stop caring what they say. Or think or do. Only what you do."

—MARCUS AURELIUS, ROMAN
EMPEROR

"A compliance with the minutiae of military courtesy is a mark of well-disciplined troops."

—MAJOR GENERAL JOHN A. LEJEUNE, U.S. MARINE CORPS

"Never forget that no military leader has ever become great without audacity."

—CARL VON CLAUSEWITZ, MILITARY STRATEGIST

"The Scouts' motto is founded on my initials. It is: Be Prepared."

—LORD BADEN-POWELL, FOUNDER OF THE BOY SCOUTS & ENGLISH SOLDIER

"Discipline is the soul of an army. It makes small numbers formidable; procures success to the weak, and esteem to all."

—GEORGE WASHINGTON,
FIRST U.S. PRESIDENT &
COMMANDER-IN-CHIEF OF
THE CONTINENTAL ARMY

"Discipline is your best friend. It will take care of you like nothing else can."

—JOCKO WILLINK,
U.S. NAVY SEAL

"You may be the boss, but you're only as good as the people who work for you."

—REAR ADMIRAL WILLIAM
LEAHY, U.S. NAVY

"I know of no single formula for success. But over the years I have observed that some attributes of leadership are universal and are often about finding ways of encouraging people to combine their efforts, their talents, their insights, their enthusiasm and their inspiration to work together."

—QUEEN ELIZABETH II,
SOVEREIGN OF
GREAT BRITAIN

II

COURAGE

COURAGE IS THE ABILITY to conquer your fears in situations where you must lead and those that follow depend on you. It is a new-found strength that brings fortune and great success by empowering you to forge through obstacles, overcome mediocrity and achieve your objective.

"Come back with your shield or on it."

                —PLUTARCH, GREEK
                          PHILOSOPHER

"Son, remember your courage with each step."

                —A SPARTAN MOTHER TO
                          HER SON

"The bended knee is not a tradition of our Corps."

                —GENERAL ALEXANDER A.
        VANDERGRIFT, U.S. MARINE
                          CORPS

"Bravery is being the only one who knows you're afraid."

—COLONEL DAVID
HACKWORTH, U.S. ARMY

"Uncommon valor was an uncommon virtue."

—CHESTER NIMITZ, FLEET
ADMIRAL OF THE U.S. NAVY

"I am not afraid . . . I was born to do this."

—ST. JOAN OF ARC

"The difference between being a coward and a hero is not whether you're scared—it's what you do while you're scared."

—SERGEANT JEFF STRUECKER,
RANGER TASK FORCE

"One man with courage makes a majority."

—ANDREW JACKSON,
U.S. ARMY

"Courage is what it takes to stand up and speak; courage is also what it takes to sit down and listen."

—SIR WINSTON S. CHURCHILL,
PRIME MINISTER OF
GREAT BRITAIN

"Courage is resistance to fear, mastery of fear—not absence of fear."

—MARK TWAIN, AMERICAN
AUTHOR

"Throughout the history of our young nation, we have seen our military go bravely into battle, armed with courage and willing to make the ultimate sacrifice."

—JOHN M. MCHUGH, U.S.
SECRETARY OF THE ARMY

"If I told you that you weren't going home until we win—what would you do differently?"

—GENERAL STANLEY
MCCHRYSTAL, U.S. ARMY

"It doesn't take a hero to order men into battle. It takes a hero to be one of those men who goes into battle."

—GENERAL H. NORMAN
SCHWARZKOPF, JR.,
U.S. ARMY

"Retreat? Hell, we just got here!"

—MARINE CAPTAIN LLOYD
WILLIAMS, ANSWERING
A MESSENGER FROM
THE FRENCH COMMANDER
AS MARINES ARRIVED
AT THE BELLEAU WOOD
SECTOR IN WWI

"True courage is being afraid, and going ahead and doing your job anyhow, that's what courage is."

> —GENERAL JOHN J. PERSHING,
> U.S. ARMY

"Courage is endurance for one moment more . . . "

> —UNKNOWN U.S. MARINE,
> SECOND LIEUTENANT IN
> VIETNAM

"Courage is rightly esteemed the first of human qualities, because it is the quality that guarantees all others."

> —SIR WINSTON S. CHURCHILL,
> PRIME MINISTER OF
> GREAT BRITAIN

"We live in an external world. Everything, you have to see it, touch it. If you can for the rest of your life, live inside yourself—to find greatness, you have to go inside."

—DAVID GOGGINS,
U.S. NAVY SEAL

"Courage: a perfect sensibility of the measure of danger, and a mental willingness to endure it."

—GENERAL WILLIAM SHERMAN,
UNION ARMY

"Bravery is the capacity to perform properly even when scared half to death."

—OMAR BRADLEY, GENERAL
OF THE U.S. ARMY & FIRST
CHAIRMAN OF THE JOINT
CHIEFS OF STAFF

"You will find dying is very easy. Living, living is the difficult thing."

—DR. HAL KUSHNER,
U.S. ARMY SURGEON &
VIETNAM CAPTIVE

"Life is a competitive endeavor."

—GENERAL DAVID PETRAEUS,
U.S. ARMY

"America was not built on fear. America was built on courage, on imagination and an unbeatable determination to do the job at hand. It's a recession when your neighbor loses his job; it's a depression when you lose yours."

—HARRY S. TRUMAN,
33RD PRESIDENT OF
THE UNITED STATES &
COMMANDER-IN-CHIEF

"Courage is going from failure to failure without losing enthusiasm."

—SIR WINSTON S. CHURCHILL,
PRIME MINISTER OF
GREAT BRITAIN

"Courage is doing what you're afraid to do. There can be no courage unless you're scared."

—EDDIE RICKENBACKER,
WWI HERO

"The only thing we have to fear is fear itself."

—FRANKLIN D. ROOSEVELT,
32ND PRESIDENT OF
THE UNITED STATES &
COMMANDER-IN-CHIEF

"Valor is a gift. Those having it never know for sure whether they have it till the test comes. And those having it in one test never know for sure if they will have it when the next test comes."

—NAPOLÉON BONAPARTE,
FRENCH MILITARY LEADER &
STATESMAN

"Great tragedy has come to us, and we are meeting it with the best that is in our country, with courage and concern for others because this is America. This is who we are."

—GEORGE W. BUSH,
43RD PRESIDENT OF
THE UNITED STATES &
COMMANDER-IN-CHIEF

"Come and take them."

—KING LEONIDAS OF SPARTA

"We've been looking for the enemy for some time now. We've finally found him. We're surrounded. That simplifies things."

—CHESTY PULLER, OFFICER,
U.S. MARINES

"Damn the torpedoes, full speed ahead!"

—ADMIRAL DAVID GLASGOW
FARRAGUT, FEDERAL NAVY

"I began revolution with 82 men. If I had to do it again, I do it with ten or fifteen and absolute faith. It does not matter how small you are if you have faith and plan of action."

—FIDEL CASTRO, CUBAN
REVOLUTIONARY & PRIME
MINISTER OF CUBA

"When life seems hard, the courageous do not lie down and accept defeat; instead, they are all the more determined to struggle for a better future."

—QUEEN ELIZABETH II,
SOVEREIGN OF
GREAT BRITAIN

III

MOTIVATION

THE ABILITY TO MOTIVATE others is a gift. Motivation is the foundation of all great acts, and it comes in the form of committed engagement and execution on certain desires, passions, and expected results. Being able motivate yourself and others is hard to define and quantify.

"The Navy has both a tradition and a future—and we look with pride and confidence in both directions."

—ADMIRAL GEORGE
ANDERSON, U.S. NAVY

"Come on, you sons of bitches, do you want to live forever?"

—GUNNERY SEARGENT
DANIEL J. "DAN" DALY, U.S.
MARINES TO THE MEN IN
HIS COMPANY PRIOR TO
CHARGING THE GERMANS
DURING THE BATTLE OF
BELLEAU WOOD IN WWI

"Live for something rather than die for nothing."

—GENERAL GEORGE PATTON,
U.S. ARMY

"We are at war with the most dangerous enemy that has ever faced mankind in his long climb from the swamp to the stars, and it has been said if we lose that war, and in doing so lose this way of freedom of ours, history will record with the greatest astonishment that those who had the most to lose did the least to prevent its happening."

—RONALD REAGAN,
40TH PRESIDENT OF
THE UNITED STATES &
COMMANDER-IN-CHIEF

"Freedom is never more than one generation away from extinction. We didn't pass it to our children in the bloodstream. It must be fought for, protected, and handed on for them to do the same."

—RONALD REAGAN,
40TH PRESIDENT OF
THE UNITED STATES &
COMMANDER-IN-CHIEF

"Freedom is the oxygen of the soul."

—MOSHE DAYAN, MILITARY
LEADER & POLITICIAN

"An action committed in anger is an action doomed to failure."

—GENGHIS KHAN, RULER OF
MONGOL EMPIRE

" . . . we shall fight on the beaches, we shall fight on the landing grounds, we shall fight in the fields and in the streets, we shall fight in the hills; we shall never surrender . . . "

—SIR WINSTON S. CHURCHILL,
PRIME MINISTER OF
GREAT BRITAIN

"I know not what course others may take, but as for me, give me liberty or give me death!"

—PATRICK HENRY, AMERICAN
FOUNDING FATHER

"The law speaks too softly to be heard amidst the din of arms."

—GAIUS MARIUS, ROMAN
GENERAL & STATESMAN

"Your days are numbered. Use them to throw open the windows of your soul to the sun. If you do not, the sun will soon set, and you with it."

—MARCUS AURELIUS,
ROMAN EMPEROR

"Every plan is a good one—until the first shot is fired."

—CARL VON CLAUSEWITZ,
MILITARY STRATEGIST

"You should reach the limits of virtue before you cross the border of death."

—SPARTAN PROVERB

"There is many a boy here today who looks on war as all glory, but, boys, it is all hell."

—GENERAL WILLIAM T.
SHERMAN, UNION ARMY

"If you're walking down the right path and you're willing to keep walking, eventually you'll make progress."

—BARACK OBAMA, 44TH
PRESIDENT OF THE
UNITED STATES &
COMMANDER-IN-CHIEF

"If you know how to shoot, and are quite ready to shoot, the chances are that you won't have to shoot."

—GENERAL JOHN J. PERSHING,
U.S. ARMY

"The Gods will take care of the King's Army."

—KING DEMARATUS AT
THERMOPYLAE

"The only easy day was yesterday."

—B.U.D.S TRAINING SLOGAN,
U.S. NAVY SEALS

"I've always said that fame is fleeting, but anonymity can last a lifetime."

—JOSEPH E. JOHNSTON, U.S.
ARMY OFFICER

"Perpetual optimism is a force multiplier."

—GENERAL COLIN POWELL,
U.S. ARMY

"Learn to be indifferent to what makes no difference."

—MARCUS AURELIUS, ROMAN
EMPEROR

"He has the most who is content with the least."

—DIOGENES, GREEK
PHILOSOPHER & SOLDIER

"We've backed off in good faith to try and give you a chance to straighten this problem out. But I'm going to beg with you for a minute. I'm going to plead with you, do not cross us. Because if you do, the survivors will write about what we do here for 10,000 years."

—GENERAL JAMES MATTIS,
U.S. MARINE CORPS

"Change will not come if we wait for some other person or some other time. We are the ones we've been waiting for. We are the change that we seek."

—BARACK OBAMA, 44TH
PRESIDENT OF THE
UNITED STATES &
COMMANDER-IN-CHIEF

IV

COMMUNICATION

DELIVERING A CLEAR AND concise message in battle, business, and everyday life is paramount. Everything from getting your troops and their equipment up on a beachhead or simply negotiating the way your cup of coffee is made at the local coffee shop is dependent on your ability to convey information speedily and accurately. Individuals who have this ability to communicate effectively get what they want— and are usually rewarded handsomely in their personal and professional pursuits.

"Do not fear the enemy, for they can only take your life. Fear the media far more, for they will destroy your honour."

—VÕ NGUYÊN GIÁP, POLITICIAN
& GENERAL IN THE VIETNAM
PEOPLE'S ARMY

"Regardless of communication between man and man, speech is a necessary condition for the thinking of the individual in solitary seclusion. In appearance, however, language develops only socially, and man understands himself only once he has tested the intelligibility of his words by trial upon others."

—FRIEDRICH WILHELM VON
STEUBEN, PRUSSIAN-
AMERICAN MILITARY LEADER

"Don't explain your philosophy. Embody it."

—EPICTETUS, GREEK
PHILOSOPHER

"Every hour, focus your mind attentively . . . on the performance of the task in hand, with dignity, human sympathy, benevolence and freedom, and leave aside all other thoughts. You will achieve this, if you perform each action as if it were your last."

—MARCUS AURELIUS, ROMAN
EMPEROR

"I must govern the clock, not be governed by it."

—GOLDA MEIR, PRIME
MINISTER OF ISRAEL

"Many words are poverty."

—SPARTAN PROVERB

"The British are coming. One if by land, two if by sea."

—PAUL REVERE,
AMERICAN HERO

"Men willingly believe what they wish."

—JULIUS CAESAR, ROMAN
EMPEROR

"A room without books is like a body without a soul."

—CICERO, ROMAN STATESMAN

"Whoever said the pen is mightier than the sword obviously never encountered automatic weapons."

—GENERAL DOUGLAS
MACARTHUR, U.S. ARMY

"Optimists study English; pessimists study Chinese; and realists learn to use a Kalashnikov."

—RUSSIAN MILITARY PROVERB

"If you want to get the most out of your men, give them a break! Don't make them work completely in the dark. If you do, they won't do a bit more than they have to. But if they comprehend, they'll work like mad."

—LIEUTENANT GENERAL
CHESTY PULLER, U.S. MARINE
CORPS

"If everyone is thinking alike, then somebody isn't thinking."

—GENERAL GEORGE S. PATTON,
U.S. ARMY

"It's not what you preach, it's what you tolerate."

—JOCKO WILLINK,
U.S. NAVY SEAL

"If you don't have a good idea of what to do next after using military force, then don't use it in the first place."

—TED LIEU, U.S. AIR FORCE &
U.S. REPRESENTATIVE

"Gratitude is not only the greatest of virtues, but the parent of all others."

—CICERO, ROMAN STATESMAN

"A sense of humor can be a great help— particularly a sense of humor about (oneself). A sense of humor is part of the art of leadership, of getting along with people, of getting things done."

—GENERAL DWIGHT D.
EISENHOWER, U.S. ARMY

"If frontline troops are unclear about the plan and yet are too intimidated to ask questions, the team's ability to effectively execute the plan radically decreases."

—JOCKO WILLINK,
U.S. NAVY SEAL

"If you talk to the animals they will talk with you and you will know each other. If you do not talk to them you will not know them and what you do not know, you will fear. What one fears, one destroys."

—CHIEF DAN GEORGE, TSLEIL-WAUTUTH NATION, BRITISH COLUMBIA, CANADA

"Combat is fast, unfair, cruel, and dirty. It is meant to be that way so that the terrible experience is branded into the memory of those who are fortunate enough to survive. It is up to those survivors to ensure that the experience is recorded and passed along to those who just might want to try it."

—BRUCE H. NORTON, FORCE RECONNAISSANCE, U.S. MARINE CORPS

"The day soldiers stop bringing you their problems is the day you have stopped leading them."

—GENERAL COLIN POWELL, U.S. ARMY

V

INITIATIVE

COMPLACENCY KILLS. A GOOD leader of people and one who acts for the collective good is able to see the great windows of opportunity and seize the moment by taking initiative. If you want to live without regret in life, make it a habit to live your life by taking massive amounts of action every waking moment. When you do this, you will begin to grow and become a wise warrior. Just do it!

"It is a good thing for an uneducated man to read books of quotations."

—SIR WINSTON S. CHURCHILL,
PRIME MINISTER OF
GREAT BRITAIN

"No guts, no glory."

—MAJOR GENERAL FREDERICK
C. BLESSE, U.S. AIR FORCE

"We bring the fight to the enemy so that they don't bring it to us."

—DAN CRENSHAW,
U.S. NAVY SEAL &
U.S. REPRESENTATIVE

"The dog that trots about finds a bone."

> —GOLDA MEIR, PRIME
> MINISTER OF ISRAEL

"Nearly all men can stand adversity, but if you want to test a man's character, give him power."

> —ABRAHAM LINCOLN,
> 16TH PRESIDENT OF
> THE UNITED STATES &
> COMMANDER-IN-CHIEF

"I was determined to fight, for I have the skills and knowledge, which I was going to put to use."

> —NAKANO TAKEKO, JAPANESE
> FEMALE WARRIOR

"A good plan violently executed right now is far better than a perfect plan executed next week."

—GENERAL GEORGE S. PATTON,
U.S. ARMY

"What you seek is seeking you."

—RUMI, PERSIAN POET

"When a dog is tied to a cart, if it wants to follow, it is pulled and follows, making its spontaneous act coincide with necessity. But if the dog does not follow, it will be compelled in any case. So it is with men too: even if they don't want to, they will be compelled to follow what is destined."

—ZENO OF CITIUM,
HELLENISTIC PHILOSOPHER

"It has always been a rule that the weak should be subject to the strong; and besides, we consider that we are worthy of our power. Up till the present moment you, too, used to think that we were; but now, after calculating your own interest, you are beginning to talk in terms of right and wrong. Considerations of this kind have never yet turned people aside from the opportunities of aggrandizement offered by superior strength."

—UNKNOWN ATHENIAN
REPRESENTATIVE TO SPARTA

"It's your road, and yours alone, others may walk it with you, but no one can walk it for you."

—RUMI, PERSIAN POET

"Always set to work without misgivings on the score of imprudence. Fear of failure in the mind of a performer is, for an onlooker, already evidence of failure . . . Actions are dangerous when there is doubt as to their wisdom; it would be safer to do nothing."

—BALTASAR GRACIAN, SPANISH ARMY CHAPLAIN

"There is a story that while Socrates was in prison, awaiting his death, he heard a man sing skillfully a song by the lyric poet Stesichoros, and begged him to teach it to him before it was too late, and when the musician asked why, Socrates replied, 'I want to die knowing one thing more.'"

—AMMIANUS MARCELLINUS, ROMAN HISTORIAN & SOLDIER

"If you don't have the power to change yourself, then nothing will change around you."

—ANWAR SADAT, 3RD
PRESIDENT OF EGYPT &
LEADER OF EGYPTIAN ARMY,
ASSASSINATED
6 OCTOBER 1981

"There are very few men—and they are the exceptions—who are able to think and feel beyond the present moment."

—CARL VON CLAUSEWITZ,
MILITARY STRATEGIST

"We make generals today on the basis of their ability to write a damned letter. Those kinds of men can't get us ready for war."

—CHESTY PULLER, U.S. MARINE

"Praise the Lord and pass the ammunition!"

—LIEUTENANT HOWELL
MAURICE FORGY, U.S. NAVY

"Battles are won by slaughter and maneuver. The greater the general, the more he contributes in maneuver, the less he demands in slaughter."

—SIR WINSTON S. CHURCHILL,
PRIME MINISTER OF
GREAT BRITAIN

"People who don't gamble aren't worth talking to."

—ISOROKU YAMAMOTO,
MARSHAL ADMIRAL OF THE
IMPERIAL JAPANESE NAVY

"You make your future. Don't hope and wait for something to drop into your lap. Make it happen."

—MASTER GUNNERY
SERGEANT GUADALUPE
DENOGEAN, U.S. MARINE
CORPS

"It is better to beg forgiveness, than ask permission."

—REAR ADMIRAL GRACE
HOPPER, U.S. NAVY

VI

DEDICATION

DEDICATION IS SIMPLY THE ability to be committed. Be it waking up early, taking care of your health, practicing proper hygiene, and dressing for the day—these simple tasks of working out, showering, brushing your teeth, and making your bed need to happen on a regular basis for you to show up for life. Warriors commit and execute. When you are dedicated to your relationships, family, and career there is not anytime for fear and worry. When you are dedicated in all areas of your life, and you have a healthy balance . . . there should be no regrets.

"Success is based off of your willingness to work your ass off no matter what obstacles are in your way."

—DAVID GOGGINS,
U.S. NAVY SEAL

"It is fatal to enter a war without the will to win it."

—GENERAL DOUGLAS
MACARTHUR, U.S. ARMY

"I only regret that I have but one life to give for my country."

—NATHAN HALE, AMERICAN
SOLDIER & SPY FOR THE
CONTINENTAL ARMY

"I only want to ride the wind and walk the waves, slay the big whales of the Eastern sea, clean up frontiers, and save the people from drowning. Why should I imitate others, bow my head, stoop over and be a slave? Why resign myself to menial housework?"

—TRIỆU THỊ TRINH,
VIETNAMESE WARRIOR &
SAINT

"Habit is stronger than nature."

— QUINTUS CURTIUS RUFUS,
ROMAN HISTORIAN

"Well-being is attained little by little, and nevertheless is no little thing itself."

—ZENO OF CITIUM,
HELLENISTIC PHILOSOPHER

"Strength does not come from winning. Your struggles develop your strengths. When you go through hardships and decide not to surrender, that is strength."

—ARNOLD SCHWARZENEGGER,
ACTOR, GOVERNOR OF
CALIFORNIA &
AUSTRIAN TANKER

"He who has equipped himself for the whole of life does not need to be advised concerning each separate thing, because he is now trained to meet his problem as a whole; for he knows not merely how he should live with his wife or his son, but how he should live aright."

—ARISTO OF CHIOS, STOIC
PHILOSOPHER

"Victory was never in doubt. Its cost was. What was in doubt, in our minds, was whether . . . the last Marine would die knocking out the last Japanese gunner."

—MAJOR GENERAL GRAVES
ERSKINE, U.S. MARINES

"No man can have a peaceful life who thinks too much about lengthening it."

—SENECA, ROMAN STOIC
PHILOSOPHER

"You must do the things you think you cannot do."

—ELEANOR ROOSEVELT,
FORMER FIRST LADY

"Nothing great is created suddenly, any more than a bunch of grapes or a fig. If you tell me that you desire a fig, I answer you that there must be time. Let it first blossom, then bear fruit, then ripen."

—EPICTETUS, GREEK STOIC
PHILOSOPHER

"The willing are led by fate, the reluctant are dragged."

—UNNAMED GREEK STOIC
PHILOSOPHER OF ASSOS

"There's no quitting, I can't have quit in me. There was never an option to stop and quit."

—MAJOR LISA JASTER, THIRD
WOMAN TO GRADUATE FROM
U.S. ARMY RANGER SCHOOL

"What then is that which is able to conduct a man? One thing and only one, philosophy. But this consists in keeping the daemon within a man free from violence and unharmed, superior to pains and pleasures, doing nothing without purpose, nor yet falsely and with hypocrisy, not feeling the need of another man's doing or not doing anything; and besides, accepting all that happens, and all that is allotted, as coming from thence, wherever it is, from whence he himself came; and, finally, waiting for death with a cheerful mind, as being nothing else than a dissolution of the elements of which every living being is compounded. But if there is no harm to the elements themselves in each continually changing into another, why should a man have any apprehension about the change and dissolution of all the elements? For it is according to nature, and nothing is evil which is according to nature."

—MARCUS AURELIUS, ROMAN
EMPEROR

"You are a woman, so be off with you; go wherever you please. I intend to die in battle, or kill myself if I am wounded."

—TOMOE GOZEN, FEMALE
SAMURAI

"Some generals consider only unilateral action, whereas war consists of a continuous interaction of opposites . . . no strategy ever survives the first engagement with the enemy."

—CARL VON CLAUSEWITZ,
MILITARY STRATEGIST

"Truth will ultimately prevail where there is pains to bring it to light."

—GEORGE WASHINGTON,
FIRST U.S. PRESIDENT &
COMMANDER-IN-CHIEF OF
THE CONTINENTAL ARMY

Good ideas are not adopted automatically. They must be driven into practice with courageous impatience. Once implemented they can be easily overturned or subverted through apathy or lack of follow-up, so a continuous effort is required.

—ADMIRAL HYMAN RICKOVER,
U.S. NAVY

"Every great dream begins with a dreamer. Always remember, you have within you the strength, the patience, and the passion to reach for the stars to change the world."

—HARRIET TUBMAN,
AMERICAN ABOLITIONIST,
ARMED SCOUT & SPY FOR
THE UNION ARMY

"Never forget: When no one else would, you raised your right hand and sacrificed, and became a part of this nation's history and Marine Corps legacy."

—CORPORAL KYLE
CARPENTER, U.S. MARINE &
MEDAL OF HONOR RECIPIENT

"The promise given was a necessity of the past: the word broken is a necessity of the present.

—NICCOLÒ MACHIAVELLI,
ITALIAN DIPLOMAT

"In every battle there comes a time when both sides consider themselves beaten, then he who continues the attack wins."

—ULYSSES S. GRANT, 18TH
PRESIDENT OF THE UNITED
STATES & COMMANDING
GENERAL OF THE
UNION ARMY

"I came here, where freedom is being defended, to serve it, and to live or die for it."

—CASIMIR PULASKI, POLISH &
AMERICAN SOLDIER

"Our land is everything to us . . . I will tell you one of the things we remember on our land. We remember that our grandfathers paid for it—with their lives."

—JOHN WOODEN LEG,
NORTHERN CHEYENNE
WARRIOR

"The spirit of our fathers arose and spoke to us to avenge our wrongs or die . . . We set up the war-whoop, and dug up the tomahawk; our knives were ready, and the heart of Black Hawk swelled high in his bosom when he led his warriors to battle."

—CHIEF BLACK HAWK,
MA-KA-TAI-ME-SHE-KIA-KIAK

VII

INTEGRITY

WARRIORS DO THE RIGHT thing even when no one is watching. You can count on them to make just decisions in a deadly battle to save the people on their left and right. Integrity is just a word until it becomes a tenet. The persons and groups embodying its proper definition can triumph over any corruption. The members serving our military are great practitioners who personify this wisdom with their many hours of education, drilling, training, and execution to reinforce good behaviors and sound decision making.

"It is not the man who has too little, but the man who craves more, that is poor."

—SENECA, ROMAN STOIC
PHILOSOPHER

"People value honesty. They value integrity. They value competence and courage and all those kinds of things."

—RICHARD A. KIDD, 9TH
SERGEANT MAJOR OF
THE ARMY

"I was in my thirteenth year when I heard a voice from God to help me govern my conduct. And the first time I was very much afraid."

—ST. JOAN OF ARC

"To live, mankind must recover its essential humanness and its innate divinity; men must recover their capacity for humility, sanity and integrity; soldier and civilians must see their hope in some other world than one completely dominated by the physical and chemical sciences."

—COLONEL GEORGE STANLEY,
CANADIAN ARMY

"The American people rightly look to their military leaders to be not only skilled in the technical aspects of the profession of arms, but to be the men of integrity."

—GENERAL JOSEPH LAWTON
COLLINS, U.S. ARMY

"Sovereign power is nothing if it does not care for the welfare of others, and it is the task of a good ruler to keep his power in check, to resist the passions of unbridled desire and implacable rage, and to realize that, as the dictator Caesar used to say, the recollection of past cruelty is a wretched provision for old age."

—AMMIANUS MARCELLINUS,
ROMAN SOLDIER &
HISTORIAN

"Those who stand for nothing fall for anything."

—MAJOR GENERAL ALEXANDER
HAMILTON, NEW YORK STATE
MILITIA

"The truth of the matter is that you always know the right thing to do. The hard part is doing it."

—GENERAL H. NORMAN
SCHWARZKOPF, JR.,
U.S. ARMY

"Painfully convinced of the unutterable wrongs and woes of slavery; profoundly believing that, according to the true spirit of the constitution and the sentiments of the fathers, it can find no place under our national government."

—SENATOR CHARLES SUMNER,
LEADER OF THE RADICAL
REPUBLICANS

"Do not swallow bait offered by the enemy. Do not interfere with an army that is returning home."

—SUN TZU, CHINESE GENERAL
& MILITARY STRATEGIST

"To sin by silence when they should protest makes cowards of men."

—ABRAHAM LINCOLN,
16TH PRESIDENT OF
THE UNITED STATES &
COMMANDER-IN-CHIEF

"There is in fact no way of correcting wrongdoing in those who think that the height of virtue consists in the execution of their will."

—AMMIANUS MARCELLINUS,
ROMAN SOLDIER &
HISTORIAN

"The nation which forgets its defenders will be itself forgotten."

—CALVIN COOLIDGE,
30TH PRESIDENT OF
THE UNITED STATES &
COMMANDER-IN-CHIEF

"Better to do a little well than a great deal badly."

—SOCRATES, GREEK
PHILOSOPHER

"We must remember that any oppression, any injustice, any hatred, is a wedge designed to attack our civilization."

—FRANKLIN D. ROOSEVELT,
32ND PRESIDENT OF
THE UNITED STATES &
COMMANDER-IN-CHIEF

"There can be no question of mistake or error raised before men who consider whatever they choose to do to be in itself the greatest of virtues."

—AMMIANUS MARCELLINUS,
ROMAN SOLDIER &
HISTORIAN

"The supreme quality for leadership is unquestionably integrity. Without it, no real success is possible, no matter whether it is on a section gang, a football field, in an army, or in an office."

—GENERAL DWIGHT D.
EISENHOWER, U.S. ARMY

"Our actions, particularly interventions, can upset regions, nations, cultures, economies, and peoples, however virtuous our purpose. We must ensure that the cure we offer through intervention is not worse than the disease."

—GENERAL STANLEY
MCCHRYSTAL, U.S. ARMY

"First learn the meaning of what you say, and then speak."

—EPICTETUS, GREEK STOIC
PHILOSOPHER

"Enjoy present pleasures in such a way as not to injure future ones."

—SENECA, ROMAN STOIC
PHILOSOPHER

"It is from numberless diverse acts of courage and belief that human history is shaped. Each time a man stands up for an ideal, or acts to improve the lot of others, or strikes out against injustice, he sends forth a tiny ripple of hope, and crossing each other from a million different centers of energy and daring, those ripples build a current that can sweep down the mightiest walls of oppression and resistance."

—ROBERT F. KENNEDY,
U.S. NAVY

"The new integrity of the world, in our view, can be built only on the principles of the freedom of choice and balance of interests."

—MIKHAIL GORBACHEV, FINAL
PRESIDENT OF THE SOVIET
UNION

"The future success of our Nation depends on our children's ability to understand the difference between right and wrong and to have the strength of character to make the right choices. To help them reach their full potential and live with integrity and pride, we must teach our children to be kind, responsible, honest, and self-disciplined. These important values are first learned in the family, but all of our citizens have an obligation to support parents in character education of our children."

—GEORGE W. BUSH,
43RD PRESIDENT OF
THE UNITED STATES &
COMMANDER-IN-CHIEF

"If you tell the truth, you don't have to remember anything."

—MARK TWAIN, AUTHOR

"Let no pleasure tempt thee, no profit allure thee, no persuasion move thee, to do anything which thou knowest to be evil; so shalt thou always live jollity; for a good conscience is a continual Christmas."

—BENJAMIN FRANKLIN,
MILITARY COMMANDER &
FOUNDING FATHER

"I don't know how I'm going to live with myself if I don't stay true to what I believe."

—CORPORAL DESMOND DOSS,
U.S. ARMY & MEDAL OF
HONOR RECIPIENT

"When you are commanding, leading [soldiers] under conditions where physical exhaustion and privations must be ignored, where the lives of [soldiers] may be sacrificed, then, the efficiency of your leadership will depend only to a minor degree on your tactical ability. It will primarily be determined by your character, your reputation, not much for courage—which will be accepted as a matter of course—but by the previous reputation you have established for fairness, for that high—minded patriotic purpose, that quality of unswerving determination to carry through any military task assigned to you."

—GENERAL GEORGE C.
MARSHALL, U.S. ARMY

"A person who is fundamentally honest doesn't need a code of ethics. The Ten Commandments and the Sermon on the Mount are all the ethical code anybody needs."

—HARRY S. TRUMAN,
33RD U.S. PRESIDENT &
COMMANDER-IN-CHIEF

"No friend ever served me, and no enemy ever wronged me, whom I have not repaid in full."

—LUCIUS CORNELIUS SULLA,
ROMAN GENERAL, SOLDIER &
STATESMAN

"Always stand on principle . . . even if you stand alone."

> —JOHN ADAMS, FOUNDING
> FATHER, 2ND PRESIDENT
> OF THE UNITED STATES &
> COMMANDER-IN-CHIEF

"Whenever you do something, act as if all the world were watching."

> —THOMAS JEFFERSON,
> FOUNDING FATHER,
> 3RD PRESIDENT OF
> THE UNITED STATES &
> COMMANDER-IN-CHIEF

VIII

FRATERNITY

A<small>LL MEMBERS OF THE</small> military share a common bond as members of the biggest and baddest fraternity in the world. A fraternity is a group of people who share the same common interests, camaraderie and similar life experiences whether that be on the training fields or in the theatre of combat. The value of fraternity lies in everyone having absolute commitment to a common cause—a total buy-in which enables them to accomplish what one person cannot.

"A spirit of comradeship and brotherhood in arms came into being in the training camps and on the battlefields. This spirit is too fine a thing to be allowed to die. It must be fostered and kept alive and made the moving force in all Marine Corps Organizations."

— MAJOR GENERAL JOHN A. LEJEUNE, U.S. MARINE CORPS

"In the military, you learn the essence of people. You see so many examples of self-sacrifice and moral courage. In the rest of life, you don't get that many opportunities to be sure of your friends."

—ADAM DRIVER, ACTOR, U.S. MARINE CORPS

"I can't expect loyalty from the army if I do not give it."

> —GENERAL GEORGE C. MARSHALL, U.S. ARMY

"A ship without Marines is like a garment without buttons."

> —ADMIRAL DAVID DIXON PORTER, U.S. NAVY

"The goal of life is living in agreement with Nature."

> —ZENO OF CITIUM, HELLENISTIC PHILOSOPHER

"Philosophers tell us that there are four cardinal virtues: self-control, wisdom, justice, and courage; and, in addition to these, certain practical gifts: military skill, dignity, prosperity, and generosity. All these Julian cultivated both singly and as a whole with the utmost care."

—AMMIANUS MARCELLINUS,
ROMAN SOLDIER &
HISTORIAN

"Waste no more time arguing about what a good a good man should be. Be one."

—MARCUS AURELIUS, ROMAN
EMPEROR

"Virtue is the health of the soul."

—ARISTO OF CHIOS, GREEK
STOIC PHILOSOPHER

"The walls of Sparta were its young men, and its borders the points of their spears."

—AGESILAUS II, KING OF
SPARTA

"From time to time, the tree of liberty must be watered with the blood of tyrants and patriots."

—THOMAS JEFFERSON,
FOUNDING FATHER,
3RD PRESIDENT OF
THE UNITED STATES &
COMMANDER-IN-CHIEF

"Man conquers the world by conquering himself."

—ZENO OF CITIUM,
HELLENISTIC PHILOSOPHER

"The mood and temper of the public in regard to the treatment of crime and criminals is one of the most unfailing tests of the civilization of any country. A calm and dispassionate recognition of the rights of the accused against the State, and even of convicted criminals against the State, a constant heart-searching by all charged with the duty of punishment, a desire and eagerness to rehabilitate in the world of industry all those who have paid their dues in the hard coinage of punishment, tireless efforts towards the discovery of curative and regenerating processes, and an unfaltering faith that there is a treasure, if you can only find it, in the heart of every man— these are the symbols which in the treatment of crime and criminals mark and measure the stored-up strength of a nation, and are the sign and proof of the living virtue in it."

—SIR WINSTON S. CHURCHILL,
PRIME MINISTER OF
GREAT BRITAIN

"You cannot exaggerate about the Marines. They are convinced to the point of arrogance, that they are the most ferocious fighters on earth—and the amusing thing about it is that they are."

—FATHER KEVIN KEANEY, 1ST
MARINE DIVISION CHAPLAIN

"For in this modern world, the instruments of warfare are not solely for waging war. Far more importantly, they are the means for controlling peace. Naval officers must therefore understand not only how to fight a war, but how to use the tremendous power which they operate to sustain a world of liberty and justice, without unleashing the powerful instruments of destruction and chaos that they have at their command."

—ADMIRAL ARLEIGH BURKE,
U.S. NAVY

"Let all men know how empty and powerless is the power of kings. For there is none worthy of the name but God, whom heaven, earth and sea obey."

>   —CNUT THE GREAT, KING
>   & MILITARY LEADER OF
>   DENMARK

"Never fear your enemy, but always respect them."

>   —GUNNERY SERGEANT JOHN
>   BASILONE, U.S. MARINES

"The people are the only legitimate fountain of power."

>   —JAMES MADISON, FOUNDING
>   FATHER, 4TH PRESIDENT
>   OF THE UNITED STATES &
>   COMMANDER-IN-CHIEF

IX

MERIT

MERIT IS SOMETHING WORTHY of recognition. An expression of excellence, usually because of a tremendous act or admirable behavior, the military recognizes merit through letters of appreciation, commendation, unit citations, and medals of the highest order. It is natural for people to want to be recognized for their accomplishments. and giving merit to one's attention provides an increased level of awareness, decorum and continued motivation.

"Your country needs you more."

—MOTHER OF MINNIE
SPOTTED WOLF, FIRST
NATIVE AMERICAN WOMAN
TO ENLIST IN THE U.S.
MARINE CORPS

"All adventures—especially into new territory—are scary."

—SALLY RIDE, ASTRONAUT &
FIRST WOMAN IN SPACE

"Having the fewest wants, I am nearest to the gods."

—SOCRATES, GREEK
PHILOSOPHER

"I can imagine no more rewarding a career. And any man who may be asked in this century what he did to make his life worthwhile, I think can respond with a good deal of pride and satisfaction: 'I served in the United States Navy.'"

—JOHN F. KENNEDY, U.S.
NAVY, 35TH PRESIDENT
OF THE UNITED STATES &
COMMANDER-IN-CHIEF

"Wise people are in want of nothing, and yet need many things. On the other hand, nothing is needed by fools, for they do not understand how to use anything, but are in want of everything."

—CHRYSIPPUS OF SOLI, GREEK
STOIC PHILOSOPHER

"I do hope that, with our performance in Ranger School, we've been able to inform those making decisions that we can handle things mentally and physically on the same level as men."

—KRISTEN GRIEST,
ONE OF THE FIRST TWO
WOMEN TO COMPLETE ARMY
RANGER SCHOOL

"I love the Corps for those intangible possessions that cannot be issued: pride, honor, integrity, and being able to carry on the traditions for generations of warriors past."

—CORPORAL JEFF SORNIG,
U.S. MARINES

"Everyone wants to win. But to truly succeed – whether it is at a sport or at your job or in life – you have to be willing to do the hard work, overcome the challenges, and make the sacrifices it takes to be the best at what you do."

—RONDA ROUSEY,
MMA FIGHTER

"I think that if females continue to come to this course that they can be encouraged by what we have accomplished, but hopefully they're encouraged by the legacy of the Rangers community as well. It was good enough to make us come. It was good enough to help force ourselves through."

—SHAYE HAVER,
ONE OF THE FIRST TWO
WOMEN TO COMPLETE ARMY
RANGER SCHOOL

"The foundation of every state is the education of its youth."

—DIOGENES THE CYNIC,
GREEK PHILOSOPHER

"I have been through a lot and have suffered a great deal. But I have had lots of happy moments, as well. Every moment one lives is different from the other. The good, the bad, hardship, the joy, the tragedy, love, and happiness are all interwoven into one single, indescribable whole that is called life. You cannot separate the good from the bad. And perhaps there is no need to do so, either."

—JACKIE KENNEDY, FORMER
FIRST LADY

"Carry out a random act of kindness, with no expectation of reward, safe in the knowledge that one day someone might do the same for you."

—DIANA, PRINCESS OF WALES

"I suggest taking the high road and have a little sense of humor and let things roll off your back."

—SALLY RIDE, ASTRONAUT & FIRST WOMAN IN SPACE

"Only the dead have seen the end of war."

—PLATO, GREEK PHILOSOPHER & SOLDIER

"Success is the result of hard work, busting your ass every day for years on end without cutting corners or taking shortcuts."

—RONDA ROUSEY,
MMA FIGHTER

"If I think I've accomplished what I set out to accomplish, then that's achievement."

—SALLY RIDE, ASTRONAUT &
FIRST WOMAN IN SPACE

"He who conquers himself is the mightiest warrior."

—CONFUCIUS, CHINESE
SOLDIER, PHILOSOPHER &
POLITICIAN

"Men are sometimes hanged for telling the truth."

—ST. JOAN OF ARC

"Only from the heart can you touch the sky."

—RUMI, PERSIAN POET

"Trust yourself. Create the kind of self that you will be happy to live with all your life. Make the most of yourself by fanning the tiny, inner sparks of possibility into flames of achievement."

—GOLDA MEIR, PRIME
MINISTER OF ISRAEL

"Stop acting so small. You are the universe in ecstatic motion."

—RUMI, PERSIAN POET

"You learn something out of everything, and you come to realize more than ever that we're all here for a certain space of time, and, and then it's going to be over, and you better make this count."

—NANCY REAGAN, FORMER
FIRST LADY

"Among American citizens, there should be no forgotten men and no forgotten races."

—FRANKLIN D. ROOSEVELT,
32ND PRESIDENT OF
THE UNITED STATES &
COMMANDER-IN-CHIEF

X

RESILIENCE

WARRIORS ARE SOME OF the most resilient members of society. They endure the difficult and have the propensity to bounce back. Warriors are flexible and rebound quickly. All too often individuals take on difficult tasks with every intention of conquering them, yet they give up and retreat at even the first signs of resistance. Building resilience will help you break through the cycle of failure and finally taste the sweet rewards of perpetual victory.

"Wait for that wisest of all counselors: time."

—PERICLES, GENERAL OF
ATHENS

"I will not be triumphed over."

—CLEOPATRA, QUEEN OF
THE PTOLEMAIC
KINGDOM OF EGYPT

"If I always appear prepared, it is because before
entering an undertaking, I have meditated long
and have foreseen what might occur. It is not
genius where reveals to me suddenly and secretly
what I should do in circumstances unexpected
by others; it is thought and preparation."

—NAPOLÉON BONAPARTE,
FRENCH MILITARY LEADER &
STATESMAN

"Anger is defined by philosophers as a long-standing and sometimes incurable mental ulcer, usually arising from weakness of intellect. In support of this they argue with some plausibility that this tendency occurs more in invalids than in the healthy, more in women than in men, more in the old than the young, more in those in trouble than in the prosperous."

—AMMIANUS MARCELLINUS,
ROMAN SOLDIER &
HISTORIAN

"Your name is unknown. Your deed is immortal."

—INSCRIPTION ON TOMB OF
THE UNKNOWN SOLDIER IN
MOSCOW

"The real man smiles in trouble, gathers strength from distress, and grows brave by reflection."

—THOMAS PAINE, AMERICAN
REVOLUTIONARY &
POLITICAL ACTIVIST

"Each man's soul is his genius."

—XENOCRATES, GREEK
PHILOSOPHER & LEADER OF
THE PLATONIC ACADEMY

"Grief is the price we pay for love."

—QUEEN ELIZABETH II,
SOVEREIGN OF GREAT
BRITAIN

"Should you see the light of your future,
within the shadows of your present,
The resilience of life dancing over vast deserts
of death,
Witness if you so shall, the majesty of Creation.
The connectedness of All was and always
will be.
Entanglement? No. We call it Love."

—SARGON OF AKKAD, SOLDIER

"A passion for life is contagious and uplifting.
Passion cuts both ways . . . I want to create
passion in my own life and with those I care
for. I want to feel, experience and live every
emotion. I will suffer through the bad for the
heights of the good."

—PAT TILLMAN, NFL FOOTBALL
STAR & ARMY RANGER, KIA

"In the midst of chaos, there is also opportunity."

—SUN TZU, CHINESE GENERAL
& MILITARY STRATEGIST

"Experience is the teacher of all things."

—JULIUS CAESAR, ROMAN
EMPEROR

"Just like in bodybuilding, failure is also a necessary experience for growth in our own lives, for if we're never tested to our limits, how will we know how strong we really are? How will we ever grow?"

—ARNOLD SCHWARZENEGGER,
ACTOR, GOVERNOR OF
CALIFORNIA &
AUSTRIAN TANKER

"Soldiers adapt. You go over there with one mind-set, and then you adapt. You adapt to the atrocities of war. You adapt to killing and dying. After a while it doesn't bother you. Well, it doesn't bother you as much. When I first arrived in Vietnam, there were some interesting things that happened and I questioned some of the Marines. I was made to realize that this is war, and this is what we do. And after a while you embrace that: This is war. This is what we do."

—KARL MARLANTES,
U.S. MARINE VETERAN

"There is no value in anything until it is finished."

—GENGHIS KHAN, RULER OF
MONGOL EMPIRE

"There's likely a place in paradise for people who tried hard, but what really matters is succeeding. If that requires you to change, that's your mission."

—GENERAL STANLEY
MCCHRYSTAL, U.S. ARMY

"When the Earth is sick, the animals will begin to disappear, when that happens, The Warriors of the Rainbow will come to save them."

—CHIEF SEATTLE [SEATLH],
SUQUAMISH CHIEF

"To save your world you asked this man to die: Would this man, could he see you now, ask why?"

—EPITAPH FOR THE UNKNOWN
SOLDIER

"We must expect reverses, even defeats. They are sent to teach us wisdom and prudence, to call forth greater energies, and to prevent our falling into greater disasters."

—ROBERT E. LEE, COMMANDER
OF THE ARMY OF THE
CONFEDERATE STATES

"Intelligence precedes operations."

—CARL VON CLAUSEWITZ,
MILITARY STRATEGIST

"It's our stuff. We made it and we know best how to use it and care for it. And now we're going to get it back."

—JOHN PRETTY ON TOP, CROW
NATIVE AMERICAN WARRIOR

"We shall live again; we shall live again."

—COMANCHE GHOST
DANCE SONG

"I hope the Great Heavenly Father, who will look down upon us, will give all the tribes His blessing, that we may go forth in peace, and live in peace all our days, and that He will look down upon our children and finally lift us far above the earth; and that our Heavenly Father will look upon our children as His children, that all the tribes may be His children, and as we shake hands to-day upon this broad plain, we may forever live in peace."

—CHIEF RED CLOUD
(MAKHIPIYA-LUTA),
SIOUX CHIEF

"Months of preparation, one of those few opportunities, and the judgment of a split second are what makes some pilot an ace, while others think back on what they could have done."

—PAPPY BOYINGTON,
U.S. MARINES

"Sometimes it takes dealing with a disability— the trauma, the relearning, the months of rehabilitation therapy—to uncover our true abilities and how we can put them to work for us in ways we may have never imagined."

—TAMMY DUCKWORTH, U.S.
ARMY & U.S. SENATE

About the Author

NICK BENAS GREW UP in Guilford, Connecticut. He is a former United States Marine Sergeant and Iraqi Combat Veteran with a background in Martial Arts (2nd Dan Black Belt in Tae Kwon-Do and Green Belt Instructor in Marine Corps Martial Arts). Nick attended Southern Connecticut State University for his undergraduate degree in Sociology, and for his M.S. in Public Policy. He has been featured by more than 50 major media outlets for his business success and entrepreneurship, including Entrepreneur Magazine, Men's Health, ABC, FOX, ESPN, and CNBC.

"Wisdom outweighs any wealth."

—SOPHOCLES, GREEK
MILITARY COMMANDER &
PHILOSOPHER

Also by Nick Benas

The Warrior's Book of Virtues
Mental Health Emergencies
Tactical Mobility